I0425573

Critics agree.

"This book is a must-read. It is invaluable in our ongoing fight against the unholy alliance of left-wing crazies and woke socialist wackos (not to mention the shape-shifting alien reptiles who control our brain waves with their advanced media mind manipulation technology)."

— Conspiracy Weekly

"A stunning achievement, a defiant slap in the face of creeping collectivist indoctrination and the Left's undeclared war on free speech and transparency. Great Joe Biden jokes too."

— The High Plains Drifter

"Never in the field of human conflict was so much owed by so many to so few for such a ridiculously low price!"

— The Times of New London, Arizona

Dedication

This book is dedicated to Al Franken, Al Gore, Al Sharpton, Alan Freeman, Alec Baldwin, Alexandria Ocasio-Cortez, Alice Walker, Alicia Garza, Alicia Keys, Alyssa Milano, Amy Klobuchar, Amy Schumer, Ana Navarro, Anderson Cooper, Andrea Dworkin, Andreas Baader, Andrew Sullivan, Angela Davis, Anna Louise Strong, Arianna Huffington, Arthur Schlesinger Jr., Barack Obama, Barbara Jordan, Bella Abzug, Bernie Sanders, Beto O'Rourke, Bette Midler, Betty Friedan, Bill Ayers, Bill Clinton, Bill Maher, Bill Moyers, Brian Stelter, Bruce Springsteen, Catharine MacKinnon, Cesar Chavez, Charles A. Beard, Charles R. Lawrence III, Chelsea Handler, Che Guevara, Cher, Cheryl Harris, Cornel West, Craig Willse, Chris Cuomo, Chris Wallace, Chrissy Teigen, Christiane Amanpour, Daniel Ortega, David Graeber, David Rieff, David Shipley, Deborah Solomon, Demi Lovato, Dennis Kucinich, Derrick Bell, Don Cheadle, Don Lemon, Earl Warren, Elizabeth Warren, Emma Goldman, Enver Hoxha, Erich Honecker, Eric Alterman, Eugene Debs, Eva Longoria, Ezra Klein, Fareed Zakaria, Fidel Castro, Fran Quigley, Frank Murphy, Fred Hiatt, Friedrich Engels, Gary Peller, Gayle King, George Clooney, George Soros, George Takai, Gerald Seib, Glenn Greenwald, Gore Vidal, Gloria Browne-Marshall, Gloria Steinem, Gudrun Ensslin, Gwyneth Paltrow, Harvey Milk, Hendrick Hertzberg, Hillary Clinton, Ho Chi-Minh, Howard Dean, Howard Stern, Hugo Chávez, Jacques Derrida, Jacques Lacan, Jake Tapper, James Comey, James Carville, James Fallows, Jane Addams, Jane Fonda, Jane Hamsher, Janeane Garofolo, Jennifer Lawrence, Jerry Brown, Jesse Jackson, Jessica Valenti, Jimmy Kimmel, Joe Biden, John Brennan, John Dewey, John Kenneth Galbraith, John Legend, John Marshall Harlan, John Powell, John Reed, Jon Stewart, Jonathan Chait, Jonathan Zasloff, Josef Stalin, Joshua Dressler, Joy Behar, Jean-Paul Sartre, Jeremy Corbyn, Jim Acosta, Judith Butler, Kamala Harris, Karl Marx, Keith Olbermann, Kevin Drum, Kim il-Sung, Kim Jong-il, Kim Jong Un, Kim Kardashian, Kimberlé Crenshaw, Kurt Andersen, Lavrentiy Beria, Lady Gaga, LeBron James, Lena Dunham, Lenny Kravitz, Leon Trotsky, Leonardo

DiCaprio, Leonid Brezhnev, Lincoln Steffens, Lionel Trilling, Louis Brandeis, Madeleine Albright, Madonna, Malcolm X, Mao Zedong, Mari Martin Sheen, Mark Ruffalo, Matsuda, Mario Cuomo, Matt Damon, Matthew Yglesias, Maureen Dowd, Mengistu Haile Mariam, Meryl Streep, Michael Harrington, Michael Moore, Michael Pollan, Michel Foucault, Michelle Obama, Mikhail Bakunin, Miley Cyrus, Nancy Pelosi, Naomi Klein, Nicolae Ceaușescu, Nicolás Maduro, Noam Chomsky, Norman Thomas, Opal Tometi, Oprah Winfrey, Patricia J. Williams, Patrisse Cullors, Paul Krugman, Paul Robeson, Pete Buttigieg, Pete Seeger, Peter Kropotkin, Peter Strzok, Pol Pot, Rachael Maddow, Ralph Nader, Reese Witherspoon, Regina Austin, Reinhold Niebuhr, Richard Delgado, Richard Hofstadter, Rob Reiner, Robert De Niro, Robert Mugabe, Robert Reich, Rosalie Abrams, Rosie O'Donnell, Russ Feingold, Ruth Bader Ginsburg, Samuel Gompers, Sarah Silverman, Saul Alinsky, Sean Penn, Seth Meyers, Slavoj Zizek, Stacey Abrams, Stephen Colbert, Stephen King, Steve Coll, Sunny Hostin, Susan Sarandon, Taylor Swift, Thomas Friedman, Thurgood Marshall, Tom Hanks, Tom Hayden, Ulrike Meinhof, Valerie Solanas, Vladimir Lenin, W.E.B. Du Bois, Walter Ulbricht, Whittaker Chambers, Whoopi Goldberg, William J. Brennan, William O. Douglas, Wolf Blitzer, Woodrow Wilson, Woody Guthrie, Yanis Varoufakis and so many, many others who could not be with us here tonight.

Think what evil creeps liberals would be if their plans to enfeeble the individual, exhaust the economy, impede the rule of law, and cripple national defense were guided by a coherent ideology instead of smug ignorance.

— P. J. O'Rourke

Contents

Preface

Much like Chairman Mao's compilation of zany one-liners published during Communist China's Cultural Revolution back in the day, this little red book is an uproarious collection of madcap humor and senseless drivel dedicated to the countless enlightened leftists still inexplicably omnipresent in our world today.

Filled with pun-ridden put-downs and wise-ass wordplay, this remarkable anthology offers unenlightened readers like yourself a thorough introduction into the baffling realm of leftist confusion and a refreshing alternative to the more conventional fare of lowbrow humor you are undoubtedly accustomed to. Your fancy will be tickled with jeering jibes and sarcastic swipes taken at the expense of the leftist elites who rule over us in relentless pursuit of a more progressive and enlightened new world order.

But just who are these enlightened leftists of the enlightened left, you ask? I'm glad you did. Enlightened leftists are those who believe that man is "perfectible" (woman too, if we stick with just two genders). They believe in equality in a world in which equality does not and cannot exist (there is no equality in nature). They are the ones who always have the "solutions" to our problems, most of these problems being, oddly, the direct or indirect result of one of their previous enlightened leftist solutions.

The enlightened left are the all too optimistic and the all too naïve with the all too good intentions. Tragically, they seem to be the only ones unaware that the road to Hell has been paved with good intentions. They are also unaware of their inherent limitations as human beings. They refuse to recognize that we are simply not able to fully understand all the ramifications of our simplest actions, much less the ambitious enlightened leftist reforms they have and repeatedly tried and will try again to introduce. They are rationalists. They are rationalists whose reason is not sufficiently able to point out the limitations of their reason.

In other words, they are the nannies, the pro-collectivist, the anti-self-reliant, the redistributors and the interventionists who have become so intrusive in our lives today. They can't accept the idea of government as *a system of negation* within which individuals can freely develop on their own under the rule of law (a "don't do this, don't do that" model – think Ten Commandments). Enlightened leftists insist that government *actively intervene* in our lives (a "do this, do that" model), always open for the next "solution" that 1) never delivers the results promised and 2) creates new problems due to the inevitable Law of Unintended Consequences.

Enlightened leftists are paternal. They are autocratic. They are above the law because what they do is for "the greater good" that they define. They believe that the ends justify the means. They are the people who say, "we are from the government and are here to help."

The enlightened left are those who refuse to leave the rest of us alone.

Although not famous for their sense of humor (telling others how to live their lives and what to think is no laughing matter), enlightened leftists nevertheless provide us with a near endless source of comic delight. This little red book is a modest attempt to tap into that vital source. I hope you will enjoy reading it. I also hope you will remember to buy a few additional copies for your friends and family. I am told it makes a wonderful gift idea, perfect, even, for any perfect or near-perfect stranger you might unexpectedly bump into on the street. It is a very small book. This makes it very easy for you to carry several of them on your person. I carry three of them with me at all times, for instance. I am sitting on two right now as I write these very lines.

In closing, please try to keep two things constantly in mind while reading: First of all, many if not most of the enlightened left mean well. Honestly. They really do. Secondly, never forget that part about the road to hell being paved with good intentions.

The Little Red Book

One of the enlightened left's abiding charms is that they truly believe themselves to be intellectually and morally superior. This superiority permits them to override any outdated traditional beliefs or moral concepts their less enlightened compatriots might still be clinging to.

*

Why did the medics rush the enlightened leftist to the emergency room? His heart had stopped bleeding.

*

What made the peacenik gardener so sure his flowers would bloom again in the spring? He knew that violets would only create more violets.

*

Why aren't progressives more worried about things getting worse? Because they are getting progressively worse.

*

Knock-knock, said the ex-feminist.
Who's there?
Mansplain.
Mansplain who?
Mansplain better at some things than woman is.

*

How are cats and Democrats similar? A cat has nine lives. A Democrat has nine votes.

*

Why do liberals love to eat donuts so much? Because they're crazy about hole foods.

*

Why did the BLM activist cross the road, and then get hit by a truck? Because red lights matter.

*

Why are socialist schoolteachers so disorganized? Because they love to see the class struggle.

*

What prevented the token woman from getting her diet coke from the soda machine? She didn't have enough quotas to pay for it.

*

Why do socialist diets never work? They are always burning other people's calories.

*

Why will the Vatican never permit Democrat cardinals to select the next Pope? Because they'll crucifix the election.

*

How did the two liberals collide on the staircase? One was going uppity while the other was condescending.

*

Why did the lost hiker have to die of starvation even though the politically correct search party passed just a few feet away from him several times? They didn't want to be accused of name-calling.

*

What kind of telephone does Joe Biden use? An iPhony.

*

What form of execution do Marxists fear the most? To die in dialectic chair.

*

What was the enlightened leftist soccer player's excuse for always overshooting the goal? It wasn't lofty enough.

*

How many Democrats does it take to change a lightbulb? Three. One to say, "change is coming," one to unscrew it and one to screw it back in again.

*

Knock-knock, said the listless vegetarian.
Who's there?
Soybean.
Soybean who?
I soybean eating a lot of tofu lately.

*

Why do you never want to wait in a row behind a group of politically correct activists? They're always bringing others into line.

*

Why did the leftist engineering company's bridges keep collapsing, eventually forcing it to go out of business? They only hired social engineers.

*

Why couldn't Fidel Castro make it as a professional baseball player? He kept overthrowing everything.

How many Greens does it take to change a lightbulb? Three. One to outlaw lightbulbs, one to shut down the local power plant and one to light a candle.

*

What is the most frequent plastic surgery procedure sought by pandering, virtue signaling leftist Hollywood celebrities? The brown-nose job.

*

While seeking more centralization,
Woke Democrats faced great frustration.
The people revolted,
The next time they voted,
And commenced with their defenestration.

*

Why are enlightened leftists such sticklers about being addressed by their proper titles? They can't live without their entitlements.

*

At what times do liberals feel their most smug and superior? At the New York Times.

Society is a product of collective decision-making. Yet enlightened leftists, in their capacity as elite social engineers, and in the name of social progress and justice, do everything in their power to remove those beneath them from the decision-making process.

*

What caused the environmental activist's low-emission hybrid automobile to roll down the hill and crash into the school bus? She had left it in carbon neutral.

*

Where do woke leftist construction workers break down and analyze buildings in an effort to discover their true significance? At a deconstruction site.

*

What is Joe Biden's favorite food? Fraud chicken.

*

Why did the woke school board personnel decide to move their students directly from first grade to third? They didn't want the children to think that they were second-class citizens.

*

Why did the feminist self-help group decide to go on a diet together? They wanted to do something about their traditional women's rolls.

*

Knock-knock, said the old pacifist.
Who's there?
Peace.
Peace who?
Peace don't make me sing "We Shall Overcome" again.

How come the Hollywood handyman's business kept booming? He had no end of woke left customers with a screw loose somewhere.

Why did the Democratic representative have to spray his hands with WD-40 several times a day? To get the grease off his palms.

Why do women find Marxists so loathsome? Because they're always revolting.

In what kind of box do Democrats like to put their stuff? The ballot box.

Why did the liberal refuse to believe the latest survey? Because it was based on conservative estimates.

Despite his utopian vision,
One poor Green was the butt of derision.
With a flash of insight,
He'd become overnight,
A proponent of nuclear fission.

When do Democrat birds fly south for the Winter? They don't. They never go near the southern border.

Why did the intersectional feminist cross the road? Because there was a major intersection there.

*

What did the woke leftist do after hearing that the culture magazine she subscribed to had committed a hate speech? She cancelled it.

*

Why is it so hard to change an enlightened leftist's mind? They refuse to leave their conformity zone.

*

What ultimately compelled the feminist to quit her job in disgust? Management finally agreed to give her equal pay for equal work.

*

How did the leftist statistician lose his job at Big Media? His statistics weren't unreliable enough.

*

Two Marxists walk into a bar. "Ouch!" the first one cried, rubbing his forehead. "See? More capitalist exploitation and social inequality!" "Damn!" cried the other one, bleeding profusely. "But the victory of the proletariat is inevitable!"

*

How many critical race theorists does it take to change a lightbulb? Three. One to take the lived experience of lightbulb racism seriously, one to turn off the power (power being a requirement of oppression) and one to replace it with a lightbulb of color less susceptible to social constructs stemming from the attitudinal dynamics and cultural values of a particular group in society.

*

When Joe Biden lies in sun, what kind of tan does he get? A charlatan.

*

Woke leftists all share this obsession,
Of seeing folks under oppression.
They bang on their drums,
Until this then becomes,
Their oppression obsession profession.

*

You know what they say about woke leftist Socialist experiments doomed to failure. They're like buses. Just wait ten minutes and another one will come along.

*

How do greens punish other greens who won't follow the party line? They put them in forest labor camps.

*

Why will Joe Biden continue to stagger and sway the way he does when he walks? Because he will never be able to go straight.

*

Why are pacifist hospitals always so full? Because they have the most patience.

*

Why is the failure rate for conflict resolution tests so high among left-wing academics? Because they make their living creating problems, not resolving them.

One of the inherent limitations of enlightened leftist intellectuals is that they are incapable of understanding that they have inherent limitations. The routine failures of their special "solutions" to the world's ills (see socialism) are always attributed to something else.

*

On what day of the week does Joe Biden get most of his work done? On Frauday.

*

Why did the enlightened leftist suddenly find himself getting shunned by all his friends? He had come out of the closet and told them that he identified as a straight white male.

*

Why did the socialist send his food back to the kitchen? The salt had not been distributed equally.

*

What finally pushed the peacenik over the edge to carry out a mass shooting spree and commit suicide? Another peacenik put on John Lennon's "Imagine" one time too many.

*

How can you tell when a subversive enlightened leftist radical is sexually aroused? He has an insurrection.

*

Why did the enlightened leftist race referee disqualify all the runners of the 100-yard sprint? Not everyone had come in first.

*

Why do socialists hate rich desserts? Because they're rich.

*

Why did the transgender cross the road? To transition to the other side.

*

What do you call an utterly disordered and mismanaged situation created by Joe Biden? A clusterfake.

*

Why do Democrats live longer than Republicans? Because they're much better at cheating death.

*

Why does Joe Biden like being president so much? Because it's the heist office of the land.

*

What was the leftist academic's biggest professional regret? He had never been able to get a doctorate in indoctrinate.

*

What do you call lewd and tasteless communist disinformation? Impropaganda.

*

Why did the woke pacifist decide to become a vegetarian? He wanted to give peas a chance.

*

How come Joe Biden never gets invited to somebody's birthday party a second time? He always takes the cake.

*

Why do trade unionists detest lightening? Because it never strikes twice in the same place.

*

Knock-knock.
Who's there?
Leftist.
Leftist who?
Leftist to want what logic will not allow.

*

Why was the tree hugger disqualified at the local "Name That Tree" competition? He had been caught reading the barkcode.

*

Why did the snowflake cross the road? To escape the harsh realities and bitter truths of this world.

*

Why was the Marxist schoolboy expelled from school? For waging class warfare.

*

When do enlightened leftists think other points of view stink? Whenever they are discenting opinions.

*

Why do socialists find dictionaries so distasteful? Because of the wealth of information found there.

*

Why did the woke leftist refuse to watch the Indianapolis 500? Because the drivers place too much emphasis on race.

*

What kind of bubble tea do leftist intellectuals drink? Bubble reality.

*

What is Joe Biden's favorite African cat? The cheatah.

*

What was it about the garrulous enlightened leftist that kept annoying all her friends? She could just never get to the finger point.

*

Why couldn't the vegan stop raving about his meal? It had been uncooked to perfection.

*

Why do feminists always cheat at poker these days? They got tired of being the fairer sex.

*

There once was a liberal named Brenda,
Who repeatedly altered her gender.
Call him her or her him,
She'd just curse and look grim,
'Cause whatever you'd say would offend her.

*

Why does left-wing cake taste so sweet? Because the frosting is always added liberally.

Today's enlightened leftist academics are obliged to say nothing as convincingly as possible. People who get to the point only make them nervous and suspicious. To actually say something defeats the purpose of their discourse as everything is relative in their postmodern dreamworld and must remain meaningless to have any value.

*

Why is it easier for liberals to lose weight? Because they are such busy bodies.

*

Two Greens walk into a bar. "Ouch!" the first one cried, rubbing his forehead. "See? Nuclear power is irresponsible!" "Hey, ow!" cried the other one, bleeding profusely. "And big polluters should have to pay more!"

*

Why do insurance companies never want to deal with Joe Biden? Because no one has lie-abilities like him.

*

What do you have to do to become a communist valedictorian? You have to get the highest Marx in your class.

*

Why did the enlightened leftist have to throw away her favorite blouse? She had worn tolerance on her sleeve too long.

*

How did the pacifist die? Peacefully, in his sleep.

*

Knock-knock, said the self-conscious green.
Who's there?
Forest.

Forest who?
Forest to choose, I'd rather not have to carry this stupid jute bag around with me all the time.

*

Why are enlightened leftists so good at giving roll calls? They're naturals when it comes to calling names.

*

What do you call the secret exchange of the next round of election fraud tactics between Democrats? The trades of the trick.

*

Why did the feminist cross the road? She had wrecked her car tying to parallel park again and had to get to work.

*

What did the woke leftist inventor say after strapping on his new flying machine and jumping off the cliff to his lamentable death? "This is MY truth! And MY physics!"

*

Why is Joe Biden's job so hard? He has a double-cross to bear.

*

A young Marxist had one sole objective,
To find a girl not so selective.
But none felt attracted,
So depressed he reacted,
By leasing one from the collective.

*

How did the gun vilifying snowflake manage to shoot himself in the foot? No one had issued him a trigger warning.

*

How many feminists does it take to change a lightbulb? Four. One to break it, one to liberate it from the socket, one to replace it with a bulb less burdened by traditional light-bulb roles and one to empower it.

*

What's the downside of having a job in the green energy sector? The contracts aren't renewable.

*

Why couldn't the communist remember the party line? He had lost his train of thought control.

*

What is Joe Biden's favorite seafood? Scampi. With extra Scam.

*

How do Chinese communists like their chicken? Golden crunchy on the outside, Maoist on the inside.

*

Why do socialists prefer light dinners? Because they're still digesting their free lunch.

*

Why did the green refuse to put the non-biodegradable waste on his refuse heap? Because he couldn't refuse it.

*

Why was the enlightened leftist so sure that things would start picking up again for him soon? He just couldn't condescend any further.

*

Knock-knock, said the frugal, hungry vegetarian.
Who's there?
Foodie.
Foodie who?
Foodie portions you get at this restaurant it's just not worth it.

*

When should you suspect your chemistry professor of being a radical leftist academic? When he adds subversive elements to the periodic table.

*

Why did the millennial have no problem marrying an older, less attractive woman? Because he saw her as his participation trophy wife.

*

How do Democrats who work at polling stations generally get along with one another? Great, practically always as thick as thieves.

Political Correctness is revenge, punishment for deeds in history directed against those who did not commit them. It willfully causes discord. It is a form of sabotage. No one can say how long these woke corrective measures will continue, however, as there is no statute of limitations for these types of "crimes."

*

Why does it take Joe Biden twice as long to shave as everybody else? Because he's two-faced.

*

What do you call an obsessive-compulsive enlightened leftist who never stops enumerating the ways in which socialism has never managed to work? A counter-revolutionary.

*

While dreaming her socialist dream world,
A leftist screamed out an obscene word.
She'd seen without doubt,
It would never pan out,
'Cause sadly our world is the real world.

*

What's the only way you can get a leftist to shut up? Wait until they have nothing left to say.

*

Where do the enlightened leftists at Moral High School play badminton? On the Moral High grounds.

*

Knock-knock, said the liberal snoot.
Who's there?
Altruist.

Altruist who?
Altruist the words around in your mouth until you talk like a liberal snoot, too.

*

How did the idealistic, first-term Democrat become so quickly disillusioned with her senior colleagues in Washington? They were all too swamped to help her.

*

Why did the enlightened leftist never have a problem getting a date? He identified as a heterosexual transgender non-binary lesbian crossdressing gay.

*

When do Democratic candidates sleep the most soundly? When they're snuggly wrapped up in cheat sheets.

*

Why did the injured progressive intellectual chide and disparage everyone he met during his short stay in the emergency room? He was in critical condition.

*

Why did the socialist psycho killer cut off the head of his victim and dissolve it along with the rest of the body in hydrofluoric acid? Because the rich weren't being taxed enough.

*

There once was a liberal snowflake,
Whose friends even thought was a fruitcake.
They felt such disgrace,
He was locked in safe space,
And kept there until it was daybreak.

Why did the progressive chemist insist on carrying out his laboratory tests in public? He was a proponent of social experiments.

*

What is Joe Biden's favorite Rolling Stones song? You Con Always Get What You Want.

*

Knock-knock.
Who's there?
Thought conformity.
Thought conformity who?
Thought conformity would be easy at first but this is really getting tedious.

*

Why did the liberal white football player lie to the high school coach about his ethnic background? He wanted to play on diversity team.

*

Why do leftists naturally avoid people with years of hard-earned experience and proven, passed-down knowledge? Because they know they can't be leftists.

*

How can you insult an enlightened leftist without causing any offense? Give him a left-handed compliment.

*

Why do enlightened leftists never have to worry about their weight like the rest of us do? Because they have already been enlightened.

Why did the radical leftist keep failing his practical driving test? He steadfastly refused to turn right.

Why is Joe Biden such a good con man? He's spent nearly fifty years in Con-gress.

How many Marxists does it take to change a lightbulb? Three. One to eradicate the light bulb as a symbol of capitalist power and privilege, one to eliminate private property and ownership of the means of production and one to ignite a torch to light the way to proletarian dictatorship.

What drove the enlightened leftist feminist to stop accepting packages for her enlightened leftist neighbor next door? She resented his mail privilege.

There once was a zero-sum cynic,
Who called the free market a gimmick.
He moaned in disdain,
That his loss was their gain,
From his post as acclaimed academic.

How did the socialist prosecutor get the proletarian defendant to plead guilty to a lesser charge? He plebian-bargained.

Enlightened leftists are obsessed with guilt. They get high on it. It is the moral intoxication that turns them from being "nobodies" minding their own business into moral supermen saving the world.

*

Why are enlightened leftists always catching drafts and getting head colds? They're too open minded.

*

What do you call an overly compassionate leftist who ceaselessly helps others who don't need any help and only want to be left alone? A Greater Good Samaritan.

*

What did Joe Biden like best about being Vice President? The vice.

*

Why did the nihilist decide to become a woke leftist? He believed he could make the void a better place.

*

How did the radical feminist electrician die in a tragic work-related accident? She had been too insistent upon taking charge.

*

Why was the enlightened leftist refused entry to the Systematic Oppression Workshop? He had forgotten to bring his identity group card.

*

What is the only standardized measure of weight that actually changes its value as the circumstances dictate? A Clin-ton.

*

When did the leftist academic realize that no one else was interested in his vision? When his psychiatrist explained to him that no one else could see it.

*

What do you call a woke leftist research institute for politically incorrect problems? A groupthink-tank.

*

Knock-knock, said the tired, old pacifist.
Who's there?
Harmony.
Harmony who?
Harmony more times are you going to make me sing "We Shall Overcome" again?

*

What does Joe Biden have after taking Viagra? A stolen erection.

*

What made the social justice warriors so reluctant about letting the new guy join their group? He was lactose intolerant.

*

There once was a bleeding-heart liberal,
Who mistakenly swallowed the red pill.
He screamed in denial,
Spewing froth, puke and bile,
'Till his bleeding heart came to a standstill.

*

What did the enlightened leftist liberal say when she stubbed her toe on a rock? Corporations should be expropriated!

Why did the newly elected enlightened leftist lesbian suddenly resign from public office in disgust and dismay? Because she had been given a mandate.

*

What kind of dog have vegetarian dog breeders still not managed to breed? Vegeterriers.

*

Knock-knock, said the communist hardliner.
Who's there?
Gulag.
Gulag who?
Gulag with your new totalitarian state.

*

How many Antifa activists does it take to change a lightbulb? Three. One to bust the old lightbulb with a baseball bat, one to replace it and one to bust the new one with a crowbar.

*

What is Joe Biden's favorite month? Ju-lie.

*

Why do liberals like fragrant candles? They want to be incensed all the time.

*

How many leftist journalists does it take to change a lightbulb? Three. One to twist the lightbulb out of proportion, one to replace it with a brazenly biased bulb and one to switch on the current with a news flash.

*

What do you call an enlightened leftist balloonist? Someone left hanging in the air.

*

What excuse did the Marxist always use to avoid engaging in class struggle? He was too busy walking his dogma.

*

Why did the enlightened leftist millennial astronaut refuse to go on his spacewalk? The space outside just wasn't safe enough.

*

Why do all masters of ceremony know to always keep Joe Biden off stage? Because otherwise he'll steal the show.

*

Why did the enlightened leftist feminist die a slow and horrible death on the battlefield while endangering her comrades in the process? She had identified as a combat soldier.

*

Knock-knock, the pacifist said.
Who's there?
The moralist.
The moralist who?
The moralist to make love, not war.

Diversity is what enlightened leftists want? The Left's control of academia, media and the entertainment industry (to name just a few) ensures intellectual orthodoxy and the power to impose it on the rest of society. This is what is called a monoculture.

*

What part of the fish do pacifists prefer to eat? The docile fin.

*

Why do woke leftists never hesitate to buy expensive luxury items? They're always seeking the greater goods.

*

Why did the vegan send his nuts and berries back to the kitchen in disgust? They had been uncooked to death.

*

Why is it a good strategy to have enlightened leftist football players on your defensive squad? They take offense so easily.

*

What do socialists love to eat? Barbeque chicken left-wings.

*

Why will Joe Biden always have a problem with personal hygiene? Because he will never come clean.

*

Why did the liberal gambler get tossed out of the poker game? He couldn't stop asking for another new deal.

*

What do sniveling leftists like to drink while they're having a bitch session? Red whine.

Why was the leftist CEO forced to take Free Lunch Inc. off the New York Stock Exchange? He had accidentally issued too many fair shares.

*

Why wasn't the introspective progressive intellectual able to pull himself away from the mirror? He couldn't get enough of his own reflection.

*

Why did the communist drown after falling into the water during an enlightened leftist boat cruise? They weren't able to reach him with the party line.

*

A leader of leftist resistance,
Was a hothead and easy to incense.
He resisted so madly,
He hurt himself badly,
And now lives off social assistance.

*

Why did the enlightened leftist find it so difficult to trust women? Because he identified as a woman.

*

What does Joe Biden do when someone accuses him of having counterfeit ideas? He forges ahead.

*

When is an enlightened leftist loneliest? When he is left alone.

*

Why was the liberal so conflict-adverse? He had a faint bleeding heart.

Knock-knock, said the conservative mother to her leftist son.
Who's there?
Big gov.
Big gov who?
Big gov your own damned socks from now on you lazy, no-good leftist. I'm not going to do it anymore!

*

Why do pacifist students do so awful on exams? They refuse to hit the books.

*

What do enlightened leftist feminists call masseurs who massage them in a particularly brutal fashion? Massageogynists.

*

Why did the enlightened leftist enjoy being offended all the time? He felt comfortable in his own thin skin.

*

Why did the peace activist refuse to get on the cop's motorcycle when he was offered a lift back into town? Because it was a cycle of violence.

*

Why does Joe Biden act so confident all the time? Because he's a confidence man.

*

Why is it a sound idea to have an enlightened leftist handle your stock market assets? Because they always make small issues into big ones.

*

Knock-knock, said the self-conscious green.

Who's there?
Prius.
Prius who?
Prius don't make me drive this car in public.

*

Which wokes are the most disagreeable? The wokes who just woke up on the wrong side of bed.

*

Why did the social justice warrior get on everybody's nerves? He was on an empower trip.

*

There once was a mean trans professor,
Who got tossed for a straight cis successor.
When he went to complain,
Said the Dean: "All's in vain,"
Your successor is quite the cross-dresser."

*

What are the only kind of fences Joe Biden is interested in? Criminal offences.

How to spot enlightened leftist elitists: 1) They call themselves anti-elitists. 2) They conform by calling themselves non-conform, all thinking the same. 3) They are in endless conflict with traditional values, seeing themselves as the avant-garde of some supra-national brave new world that nobody else wants but them.

*

Why did the enlightened leftist ecologist find it so difficult to mingle at the WWF cocktail party? He was a lousy conservationist.

*

Why did the university applicant feel he was being treated unfairly when he was not admitted based on his racial background but the applicant with the same racial background was? He knew he was just as undeserving of admission as the other guy.

*

Why enlightened leftist refuse listen lecture? Because he hate speech.

*

Why had the seasoned social reformer become so despondent? He felt he was now just the shadow of his reformer self.

*

Why was the hand-wringing leftist always so much quicker at expressing his misgivings than the others? He always used the express concern lane.

*

What do you call a mind reader who advocates protecting our precious natural resources from exploitation and pollution? An environ-mentalist.

*

What makes millennial men such whiney, self-centered narcissists? Their generation Y chromosome.

*

What kind of rock bands do enlightened leftist union members prefer listening to? It doesn't really matter as long as they're special interest groups.

*

Why does Joe Biden have so much trouble putting away his pen after signing executive orders? Because thinking about the pen always make him nervous.

*

How did the enlightened leftist feminist ruin her back during her first week on the job? She had identified as a furniture removal man.

*

How come the enlightened leftist esoteric never bothered to patch up the rips in her socks? She was a firm believer in holism.

*

Old Jane was a fierce gun controller,
So hysterical none could console her.
She would spew, screech and shout,
'Till her doctor found out,
She was really severely bi-polar.

*

Why did the eco-sexual change his partners so often? He wanted more biodiversity.

Why do swindlers everywhere admire Joe Biden? Because he thinks outside the box of tricks.

*

How has virtue signaling become such a dangerous endeavor for left-wing Hollywood celebrities to undertake? They fall over themselves trying to do it.

*

Why did the Democrat love to drive in the mountains so much? Because the roads there are so crooked.

*

Why was the green activist so eager to undergo liposuction? She was a strong advocate of waist management.

*

Why are enlightened leftists so quick to shake hands? They're always on the lookout for a hand out.

*

Knock-knock, said the limping peacenik.
Who's there?
Peace march.
Peace march who?
Peace march a little more to the right, will you? You keep stepping on my foot.

*

Why can't an enlightened leftist elitist ever lose any weight? Because elite anything.

*

What kinds of films do enlightened leftist union members love to watch? Collective action movies.

*

In what kind of city does Joe Biden always feel at right at home? In Duplicity.

*

How did the unemployed leftist professor lose his next job at the stadium entry control point? He let everybody pass.

*

What do tree-huggers call the crime of having turned your back on the tree-hugging cause? Treeson.

*

There once was a liberal named Beatrice,
Who beguiled as a forthright idealist.
But false to the core,
She was really no more,
Than your commonplace cynical nihilist.

*

When did the enlightened leftist environmentalist realize that he was now part of the green rank and file? When he looked into the toilet and saw his grass roots movement.

What do activist judges, politically biased professors, advocacy journalists and liberation theologians all have in common? They want specific results for specific groups and thus fail to do their duty.

*

How did the pacifist criminal manage to break into the cash register? By using peace-keeping force.

*

When is the only time a Democratic congresswoman stops telling lies in her dreams? When she lies awake.

*

Why did every building the woke leftist architect design end up as a catastrophic collapse? Because he always miscalculated the tolerance levels of the structures.

*

What position did Joe Biden play on his high school football team? Wide deceiver.

*

After having quit everything else he had ever tried before, what did the lethargic enlightened leftist do-gooder decide to become? An activist.

*

How did the feminist boxer lose her championship crown? She wasn't looking out for the other woman's rights.

*

Knock-knock, said the big city green.
Who's there?
Soy milk.
Soy milk who?

Soy milk this cow here to get the milk to come out, or what?

*

What is Joe Biden's favorite Microsoft product? Excel. He's an expert with spreadcheats.

*

What do you call a smiling enlightened leftist environmentalist who obsessively repeats everything you say to him? Echo-friendly.

*

Why are Greens always late for their appointments? Because they live behind the times.

*

What do moralistic high school teachers do whenever they can't agree on the proper course of politically correct action to take? They call in the moral principal.

*

What mythical large and hairy humanlike creature expressing unfashionable conservative views do leftists believe in? Bigotfoot.

*

How come the social justice warrior never went to any demonstrations during the week? He was a social justice weekend warrior.

*

Why did the enlightened leftist green have to look for a new all-natural biodegradable deodorant? Because he had bio.

What is Joe Biden's favorite type of short coat? A fleece jacket.

Why did the enlightened leftists indignantly lament the bleak future of our foredoomed planet? They wanted to make the world a bitter place.

Why wasn't the enlightened leftist union member able to present his wife with his latest list of household grievances? She had imposed a lockout.

Why did the left-wing pilot decide to make an unscheduled landing? Because the right wing had started to give him problems.

How many enlightened leftist transgender women did it take to beat the other women at the wrestling match? One.

Knock-knock.
Who's there?
Thought crime.
Thought crime who?
Thought crime couldn't get any worse under an enlightened leftist government like this but boy oh boy was I ever wrong.

Why do women avoid dancing with leftists? Because they have two left feet.

What do pacifists call their sex organs? Gentles.

*

Why are enlightened leftists so certain that their negative views on traditional values are correct? Because they're absolutely positive about them.

*

Why did the Antifa activist cross the street? To burn down the buildings on the other side.

*

What do you call a timid Democrat? A shyster.

*

What does Joe Biden do after a long day of lying to the American people from the Oval Office? He goes upstairs to lie in bed.

*

Why did the worried mother insist that her enlightened leftist son take a second portion of dinner? He was nothing but thin skin and bones.

*

In their efforts to stem exploitation,
Anxious liberals kept raising taxation.
The voters got sore,
Then rebelled and therefore,
This led to their job termination.

For conservatives, government is an end. For liberals, government is a means to an end. Conservatives are here. Leftists are "progressing." Where are they progressing? To what? They can't or won't tell you. And if they can't draw the line, there can only be one destination: The totalitarian state.

*

How did the enlightened leftist player get promoted to the varsity leftist self-esteem team? He was a regular top scorer in the blame game.

*

Knock-knock, said the skeptical free thinker.
Who's there?
Doctrine.
Doctrine who?
Doctrine around on this socialist nonsense still ain't never gonna make it work.

*

What do you call a Social Democrat who is selfish, egocentric and inconsiderate of others? An Asocial Democrat.

*

In what parallel universe does Joe Biden live in? No one knows but it's a different space-time con-tinuum.

*

Why do left-wing moralists like to spend so much time up on the moral high ground? They just love the cynic view.

*

Why do liberals insist on watching the original versions of foreign films? They have a sense of subtitlement.

*

Why are progressive women so awful at parallel parking? They are much too forward-looking.

*

Where will you find enlightened leftist mind-controlled sailors? On their censorship

*

What do you call a pacifist who diligently says no to everything in a very meticulous and exact manner? A conscientious objector.

*

Why did the environmentalist start to panic after being lost in the woods for three days? He couldn't find deforestation.

*

What do you call drunken enlightened leftist who never stops griping and moaning? A whine-o.

*

Knock-knock, said the communist revolutionary.
Who's there?
Zealot.
Zealot who?
Zealot quick before we make it communal property and you won't be able to zealot anymore.

*

When's the only time a leftist gets it right? When he's got nowhere left to go.

*

Why did the enlightened leftist turn down the LSD? He didn't think his consciousness could be raised any higher.

*

What is the only kind of jury Joe Biden feels comfortable with? Perjury.

*

What do you call the illegal buying and selling of securities by enlightened leftist political dissidents acting on privileged information? Inciter trading.

*

Why did the enlightened leftist Hollywood celebrity have to cancel her participation at the gun control rally? Her heavily armed bodyguards advised against it.

*

Why did the feminist send out nastygrams every Christmas to all of the men she knew? Because they were on her hate male list.

*

There once was a thoughtcrime detective,
Whose methods were less than effective.
He started to brood,
And was forced to conclude,
That his own thoughts were highly defective.

*

What did the pacifist order at the diner? A cup of coffee and appease of pie.

*

How did the peacenik express his pent-up hostility at the sit-in? Through pacifist-aggressive behavior.

What does Joe Biden do when he makes a decision? He puts his robber stamp on it.

*

Why are enlightened leftists so distrustful of reporters who don't work for CNN? Because many of their reports are unconformed.

*

What form of PTSD is common among most Democrats today? The Post-Trump Stress Disorder.

*

Why are some enlightened leftist ecologists so painfully shy? Because they are environmentally self-conscious.

*

Why did the feminist end her fling with a girlfriend and start up a heterosexual relationship again? She was tired of the weaker sex.

*

How many postmodernists does it take to change a lightbulb? Three. One to ask, "What is change and who's to say if change is any good?" one to say, "That thing you call a 'lightbulb' is merely an objectified expression of subjective idealism" and one to ask, "Can't we just deconstruct it instead?"

It's easy for the morally outraged to demand human rights, social justice, equality, diversity, etc. Much more difficult, if not downright offensive to many, is to demand discipline, self-control, hard work, abstinence, etc. That would entail personal consequences and responsibility and that's too much to ask.

*

What do enlightened leftists never get tired of eating? Leftovers.

*

What do enlightened leftist teachers call a B+? The greater good.

*

Who is the only psychoanalyst who could possibly help Joe Biden? Dr. Sigmund Fraud.

*

How did the peacenik justify his defecation on the steps of the Pentagon? He claimed it was his protest movement.

*

What do you call socialist countries where the populations have been well-trained to follow the party line? Indoctrinations.

*

Why is it clear to Joe Biden that he must one day stop his thieving ways? He knows that even he can only take so much.

*

Why did the enlightened leftist refuse to give his son the present he wanted for Christmas? The batteries were not inclusive.

*

In which state are Democrats regarded the most highly? In the Welfare State.

*

Why do enlightened leftists revel in dividing the country into vicious little groups and setting them upon each other? Because they believe that diversity will bring us together.

*

Why did the enlightened leftist janitor quit his job after being assigned floor cleaning duties for the third week in a row? He felt he was being mopped.

*

Why was it so hard for the enlightened leftist to take personal responsibility for the latest social ill? He had misplaced his misplaced guilt.

*

How many transgenders does it take to change a lightbulb? Three. One to reverse it from its cis-ocket, one to replace it with a non-binary, gender-confirming bulb (the same lightbulb will do) and one to switch the switch.

*

Two Democrats walk into their favorite bar. "Ouch!" the first one cried, rubbing his forehead. "Somebody lowered our bar!" "Ow!" cried the other one, bleeding profusely. "Nah. It's always been that low."

*

Where did the founders of Black Lives Matter end up once the movement had served its purpose? In Big Luxurious Mansions.

*

Why are enlightened leftists so quick to start yelling whenever they argue with their opponents? Because they hate speech.

*

What do you call a grasping environmental activist begrudging of other activists' good fortune? A green with envy.

*

What kind of watch does Joe Biden like to wear? He doesn't care as long as it stainless steal.

*

Two postmodernists walk into a bar. "Ouch!" the first one cried, rubbing his forehead. "See? That was merely a subjective objectification of a value that is relative and completely dependent on the intentionality of the observer." "Damn!" cried the other one, bleeding profusely. "I can't argue with that, but somebody ought to deconstruct that thing immediately!"

*

What do hardcore feminists make their chili con carne with? Lesbeans.

*

How come the enlightened leftist always got caught on the wrong foot? Because he had two left feet.

*

Why did the snowflake refuse to park his car in the empty parking lot? None of the parking spaces felt safe enough.

*

Knock-knock, said the Cuban communist.
Who's there?
Infidel.
Infidel who?
Infidel we trust.

*

What do you call a left-wing radical who has lost all his fervor and now ekes out a living as a disillusioned bartender? A behind-the-counterrevolutionary.

*

What do politically correct golfers call the numerical measure of their potential playing ability based on the tees played for a given course? Their disability.

*

How did the enlightened leftist get her driver's license revoked? She refused to discriminate between yellow, green and red.

*

In what capacity does Joe Biden exercise command over the United States Armed Forces? As Commander-N-Thief.

*

What do you call really vicious and savage socialist factory workers? The means of production.

*

How did the politically correct sister explain to the police why her brother was always getting into trouble? She said he was the Afro-American sheep of the family.

Woke social justice warriors are routinely shocked to discover that great historical figures fail to meet their more enlightened level of antifa, gender-theoretical, anti-racist and anti-capitalist consciousness today and therefore ravage the memory of their monumental achievements accordingly.

*

Why did communist chic have no alternative but to go out of style? It didn't have any revolutionary class.

*

What do the politically correct all have in common? They are always politically correcting something that isn't broken.

*

What led to the enlightened leftist democrat's addiction to pain pills? His chronic sore losing condition.

*

Why is it so easy to skin an enlightened leftist cat? Because its skin is so thin.

*

Why did Joe Biden never once consider becoming a bartender? Because the thought of being behind bars gives him the creeps.

*

How many lefty Hollywood celebrities does it take to change a wall mirror? Three. One to remove the old mirror and stare into it for hours, one to hang up the new mirror and one to remove its protective cover and stare into it for hours along with the celebrity who hung it up.

*

Why is it that you will rarely find a communist with a dirty mind? Because of all the brainwashing that has taken place.

Why are liberal colds so hard to shake? Because they keep getting progressively worse.

*

With what language can all leftist radicals communicate with? They all speak fluent Fringe.

*

How come the progressive fell off the high-rise during a break at the big social reform convention? He was too forward-leaning.

*

Why was the enlightened leftist constantly distracted? He was absorbed in thought control.

*

Where do combatant socialist belligerents like to sleep? In militents.

*

Knock-knock.
Who's there?
Idealist.
Idealist who?
Idealist taking responsibility for your actions and taking charge of your life without expecting any handouts from others.

*

How is Joe Biden planning to make the postal system more inclusive? By introducing more blackmail.

*

What did the illegal immigrant say once he finally reached a sanctuary city? "Holy moly! I just stepped in a pile of human shit!"

*

What do you call a hastily organized coup d'état? A rushin' revolution.

*

What did the enlightened leftist tree hugger say when his favorite tree finally blossomed? "I thought he would never leaf."

*

Why did the overly eco-aware environmentalist find his humus humiliating? Because it was biodegrading.

*

Why can a feminist revolution never take place? Because they would have to wait until everyone finishes using the bathroom first.

*

When does a leftist put his best foot forward? When reaching out his hand for a government handout.

*

Why did the communist ask for a band-aid? Because he had stubbed his manifestoe.

*

How come the green's wall sockets always made strange sounds that kept him up at night? His energy was squeaky-clean.

*

Why does Joe Biden like trees so much? Because they're so shady.

*

There once reigned a reform fanatic,
Whose change for change's sake caused a panic.
It soon rained down scorn,
On reform to reform,
And his fall from grace proved quite dramatic.

*

When did the enlightened leftist finally wake up and start smelling the coffee? After having a strong cup of harsh reali-tea.

*

Why couldn't the undercover green tell his friends about his car's ghastly exhaust problem? He saw it as a secret emission.

*

Knock-knock, said the old pacifist.
Who's there?
Sit-in.
Sit-in who?
Sit-in on my ass all day like this is really starting to get boring.
Can we start peace marching again?

It's not the greater society you belong to, it's the "oppressed" minority or hyphenated identity group du jour you belong to that matters. This somehow ennobles you, gets you the attention you so desperately need and deserve and puts everyone else on the moral defensive.

*

What made the pacifist so sure that April would be tranquil? The peace March before it.

*

How come Democrats never get lost in gusty storms? Because they go any way the wind blows.

*

Where will the enlightened leftist brain police put you if you refuse to be politically correct? In a politically correctional facility.

*

What do all socialist baseball players have in common? They're all lefties.

*

What kind of auto always does Joe Biden find the most exciting? Grand theft auto.

*

What's another name for polite privileges, courteous entitlements and amiable rights? Civil liberties.

*

What do you have when workers revolt and go on strike as beach bums in California? Labor surfdom.

*

Why did the green forget to buy her vegan cheese while shopping at the organic supermarket? She had failed to put it on her environmentalist.

*

How come the politically correct enlightened leftist felt compelled to sit down on the toilet whenever he had to urinate? He was under a lot of pee-er pressure to do so.

*

How many diversity obsessed social justice warriors does it take to change a lightbulb? No one knows because it's never been done. All lightbulbs, whatever their condition, are unique and special and irreplaceable in their own way.

*

Why can't government interrogators ever get any valuable information out of the captured "resistance" activists they interrogate? None of them know what it is they're resisting against.

*

Why wasn't the communist insurgent allowed entry to the revolutionary celebration? He wasn't on the socialist.

*

Why did Joe Biden excel at baseball as a young man? Because nobody could steal bases like him.

*

How come the enlightened leftist woman suddenly lost all interest in feminism? She finally found a man who understood her gender gap.

*

How do enlightened leftists determine the winner of an America-bashing contest? Whoever has the highest number of finger points wins.

*

Why was the woke leftist sailor never able to obtain help for her sinking ship and disappeared below the waves forever? The only distress signal she knew was the virtue signal.

*

Why did the enlightened leftist referee refuse to call players out of bounds? He was a firm believer in open borders.

*

Knock-knock, said the lisping ecologist.
Who's there?
Bike path.
Bike path who?
Just bike path the thoybean plant and turn right. You can't mith it.

*

How many enlightened leftist transsexuals does it take to form a line? Enough to make a transformation.

*

Why did the phone company turn off the socialist's telephone? Because he had stopped paying for his radicalls.

*

What musical instrument did Joe Biden play in his high school marching band? The steal drum.

*

Why did the communist third grader have to be transferred to another school? Because of all the agitation he had made in class.

*

Why do the politically correct find setting standards so tedious? They always have to set them twice.

*

What did the enlightened leftist realize with dismay after reaching for his wallet at the peace rally? Another enlightened leftist had just enlightened him of $200.

*

What kind of Marxists never take anything seriously? Groucho Marxists.

*

There once was a senile old Democrat,
Who hardly could tell you where he was at.
But he'd lie and he'd cheat,
Cover up and browbeat,
More expertly than you'cud shake a stick at.

*

What did the enlightened leftist prankster call his uncle's new conservative wife? An aunti-fascist.

Enlightened leftists believe that the failings of human nature can be "solved" and injustice eradicated. The less enlightened like you and I, however, understand that human nature is a given and must be kept in check within a system that permits the least injustice possible.

*

Why don't black people generally like to hang out with enlightened leftist liberals? Because they don't want to have to listen to black music that black people don't listen to anymore.

*

Why did Hillary fail to find the time to meet with the wife of a foreign dignitary? Because that woman's only recommendation was having been married to somebody.

*

Why does Joe Biden never want to leave Washington, D.C.? Because it's deceit of government.

*

Politically correct quiz: What do Superperson, Spiderperson and Batperson all have in common? They all have super powers.

*

Where did the communist book his first Caribbean cruise? On a comradeship.

*

There once was a liberal so thin-skinned,
His social work soon took a tailspin.
No matter who'd greet him,
He'd act like they'd beat him,
Now sacked, he's a social work has-been.

*

What was the name of the first ever Russian bowling team to advocate the immediate and forceful seizure of power by the proletariat? The Bowlshevists.

*

Why did the tree hugger decide to climb up his tree one day? He felt it was time to move on to a new branch of work.

*

Knock-knock, the feminist said.
Who's there?
The sexes.
The sexes who?
The sexes good, even if you have to do it with a man.

*

For what will Joe Biden be remembered? As having set the heist standards for future presidents of the United States.

*

How come the transsexual was thirsty all the time? He was low on gender fluid.

*

What did the woke leftist social engineer exclaim when one of his countless social engineering plans finally appeared to be working? "It's too greater good to be true!"

*

Why do rank-and-file socialists avoid socialists from Harvard? They didn't have any working class.

*

What technique finally helped the enlightened leftist union member attain inner peace and tranquility? Transcendental Mediation.

*

How come the politically correct running back decided to retire from professional football? He just couldn't bring himself to step on other people's toes anymore.

*

What did the enlightened leftist doctor find most irritating about his comatose patient? He wasn't able to raise his consciousness.

*

Why did the do-gooder get fired from his job at the equal opportunity office? They found a do-better.

*

When Joe Biden wishes for something really, really bad, what does he do? He double-crosses his fingers.

*

What do you call potatoes used by communists to help upset the status quo? Agitaters.

*

What made the enlightened leftist moralist so angry after finding out that her enlightened leftist neighbor had gone to the mega-sale at the local mall without her? She didn't share her values.

*

What do the politically correct call a president who has much less influence due to his rapidly approaching end of tenure? A physically challenged duck.

*

Why did the communist man stay at the YMCA? Because he was a fellow traveler.

*

How come the enlightened leftist ecologist's organic peanut butter and jelly sandwich left such an awful stain in his sandwich wrapper? He had made it with hole-wheat bread.

*

What do you call mines that communist sympathizer miners dig? Undermines.

*

Why do the politically correct feel uneasy using the term no-brainer? Because it's bound to offend those who don't have one.

*

How did the assertive young vegan manage to break his hand? By pounding his fist on the vegetable.

*

What is Joe Biden's favorite Elton John song? Racket Man.

*

What do you call a feminist prostitute? A pro-woman.

When conservatives are confronted with the views of liberals, they are intellectually puzzled. When liberals are confronted with the views of conservatives, they are morally outraged.

*

Why are enlightened leftist pacifists always sticking their noses into other people's business? Because they want appease of the action.

*

Why did the postmodernist cross the road? To emphasize the subjective nature of the world as opposed to any mind-independent reality and thus demonstrate that the social construct "road" cannot be objectified by crossing, not crossing, or even observing the postmodernist who just crossed it.

*

What do socialists with speech impediments have? Socialisps.

*

Why are communists generally prepared to lend other communists a helping hand? Because one brain washes the other.

*

What kind of posters work best for Joe Biden's election campaigns? Imposters.

*

What was the overweight enlightened leftist dying to try from the all-you-can-eat buffet? Anything that was left.

*

How did the woke leftist electrician die tragically on the job. He forgot to disempower the old circuit before empowering the new one.

*

What led the enlightened leftist hipster to strut around Starbucks even more obnoxiously than usual? He had just won the local Irony Man competition.

*

Why does everybody say that Joe Biden has no conviction? Because he hasn't been brought to court yet.

*

Why did the affluent enlightened leftist couple purchase a second apartment in the poor neighborhood? They wanted to take a stand against the rising gentrification problem there.

*

Knock-knock, said the enlightened leftist organic freak.
Who's there?
CO2.
CO2 who?
CO2morrow at the compost heap.

*

There once was a Democrat nation,
Obsessed with increased regulation.
It passed laws, acts and rules,
'Till this nation of fools,
Declined into disintegration.

*

Where did the Confederation of Enlightened Leftist Prostitutes draw the line when it came to oral sex? The member had to be a union member.

*

Why do green model airplanes always fall apart? Because they are glueton-free.

*

If Joe Biden is neither right-handed nor left-handed, what is he? Red-handed.

*

Why did the enlightened leftist feminist have to suffocate miserably in the pitch-black darkness after a cave-in? Because she had identified as a coal miner.

*

How do pacifists wash their clothes? With a wishy-washing machine.

*

How can you tell when a communist has had too much to drink? He loses class consciousness.

*

Knock-knock, said the socialist.
Who's there?
Free lunch.
Free lunch who?
If free lunch together will you pay for mine?

*

What was the enlightened leftist ecologist's favorite sex position? The zero emissionary position.

*

What type of businesses do enlightened leftists excel at? Anybody's business but their own.

*

What led the do-gooder to be ostracized by the rest of the do-gooders in the do-gooder group? They had caught him trying to do better.

*

How can you tell when an enlightened leftist is having a particularly bad day? When he threatens to move to Canada again.

*

What is Joe Biden's philosophy? You have to take whatever low life gives you.

*

What do you call never-ending, loud and bogus Democrat BS? A cacaphony.

*

Why did the socialist insurgents leave the rebellion in disgust? They found the other demonstrators revolting.

*

Why did the enlightened leftist union members have to go hungry during the football game? Because nobody was willing to make any concessions.

*

What is the one substance in the universe that can weaken Superman's ability to tell the difference between a normal lie and absolute horse shit? Clintonite.

If the rules of the foot race are fair, the results are fair, regardless of who wins. Enlightened leftists won't accept this, however. They keep trying to engineer a race in which everybody comes in first - or last, depending upon how you look at it.

*

What kind of Gore-Tex continues to provide waterproof protection and breathable comfort even when the global warming debate fails to develop as planned? Al-Gore-Tex.

*

How do you get on the wrong side of an environmentalist? By getting on his carbon dioxide.

*

When does Joe Biden know he can't con his way out of a situation? Whenever he's con-stipated.

*

Why did the enlightened leftist tree hugger have to stop hugging his tree after nearly a year? He was forced to take his annual leaf.

*

Why do enlightened leftists never get around to masturbating? Because they are self-satisfied to begin with.

*

What do you call an assertive pacifist? Somebody who meeks it happen.

*

Why did the socialist collective have to break up? They didn't have anything in commune anymore.

*

Knock-knock, said the defensive green.
Who's there?
Soybean.
Soybean who?
Soybean eating fast food lately. Got a problem with that?

*

How did the enlightened leftist environmentalist finally convince her husband to start using Viagra? She said it would help in the struggle for sustainable energy.

*

Why did the green waiter always crash into his colleagues whenever he entered the kitchen? He just couldn't resist the great outdoors.

*

Who is Joe Biden's favorite Mark Twain character? Hucksterberry Finn.

*

What is the only minority group that the politically correct are not worried about offending? The intelligent.

*

What did the young enlightened leftist peacenik tell his mother when he came home with a bloody nose? He had gotten into a pacifist fight.

*

Why is it never a problem to come late for an appointment with Joe Biden? Because he holds up everybody before you get there anyway.

Why do liberals like big government so much? They have a soft spot in their hearts for non-profit organizations.

*

Why was the guest at the organic restaurant startled when her meal started making strange moaning sounds? No one had warned her that it was local groan food.

*

Why did the enlightened leftist ecologist go around saying "Hello! Hello! Hello!" to everyone all of the time? He was trying to be echo-friendly.

*

Knock-knock, the communist said.
Who's there?
Police state.
Police state who?
Police state where you'll be staying while in town so we can ask you some more questions later.

*

What do you call a creepy Democrat who counts votes in such a way that it sucks the life blood out of our democratic system? A Democrat Vote Count Dracula.

*

What do you call a government-organized marathon? A state-run.

*

A real enlightened leftist never "takes a dump" when going to the bathroom. He enlightens himself.

*

What is Joe Biden's favorite breakfast cereal? Frosted Fakes.

*

Knock-knock, said the freeloading progressive.
Who's there?
Commie.
Commie who?
Commie what you want but don't commie late for dinner.

*

What did the crestfallen enlightened leftist say after finally losing a re-election? "All greater good things must come to an end."

When enlightened leftists talk about "social justice" they mean justice for particular groups. By favoring particular groups, however, they ensure that others are treated unfairly. There is no such thing as social justice. Justice is inherently social and can't play favorites.

*

Why did the enlightened leftists cross the road? To redistribute the wealth, to abolish the family, to do away with gender, to keep the masses trapped in their dependent economic state, to take over what has traditionally been the duty of communities, to sexualize children, to openly subvert American elections, to disarm the populace, to divide society into hyphenated, make-believe identity groups... To, well. To name just a few.

*

Will Joe Biden's lying finally come to end when he dies? No. Even then he will lie in state.

Random Inspirational Quotes

Ninety percent of the politicians give the other ten percent a bad reputation.

— Henry Kissinger

*

The state is that great fiction by which everyone tries to live at the expense of everyone else.

— Frederic Bastiat

*

The problem with socialism is that you eventually run out of other people's money.

— Margaret Thatcher

*

Socialism in general has a record of failure so blatant that only an intellectual could ignore or evade it.

— Thomas Sowell

*

Anyone who has visions should go to the doctor.

— Helmut Schmidt

*

The first thing a man will do for his ideals is lie.

— J. A. Schumpeter

*

Idealist: a cynic in the making.

— Irving Layton

*

Liberals are good at catchphrases, but there's no substance behind them.

— Matt Bevin

*

A liberal is a man who will give away everything he doesn't own.

— Frank Dane

*

A conservative is a liberal who got mugged the night before.

— Frank Rizzo

*

The most radical revolutionary will become a conservative the day after the revolution.

— Hannah Arendt

*

What people want is big government that they don't have to pay for.

— Timothy Noah

*

So much of left-wing thought is a kind of playing with fire by people who don't even know that fire is hot.

— George Orwell

*

I am repelled by the idea of professors in a university turned statesmen.

— John Randolph

*

You're an idealist, and I pity you as I would the village idiot.

— Stanley Kubrick

*

The function of socialism is to raise suffering to a higher level.

— Norman Mailer

*

Intellectuals study more the reputation of their own wit, than the success of another's business.

— Thomas Hobbes

*

The intellectual's hostility to the market and contempt for ordinary people are two sides of the same coin.

— Lord Peter Bauer

*

The wisest and most experienced are generally the least credulous.

— Adam Smith

*

If men were angels, no government would be necessary.

— James Madison

*

In general, the art of government consists of taking as much money as possible from one class of citizens to give to another.

— Voltaire

*

Government, even in its best state, is but a necessary evil; in its worst state, an intolerable one.

— Thomas Paine

*

The whole aim of practical politics is to keep the populace alarmed — and hence clamorous to be led to safety — by menacing it with an endless series of hobgoblins, all of them imaginary.

— H.L. Mencken

*

If you put the federal government in charge of the Sahara Desert, in 5 years there'd be a shortage of sand.

— Milton Friedman

*

Education does not make you smarter.

— Aleksandr Solzhenitsyn

*

Universities are places where fashionable but insignificant words flourish.

— Thomas Hobbes

*

A person who reads a great deal, almost the whole day, gradually loses the ability to think for himself; just as a man who is always riding at last forgets how to walk. Such, however, is the case with many men of learning: they have read themselves stupid.

— Arthur Schopenhauer

*

Education is an admirable thing, but it is well to remember from time to time that nothing that is worth knowing can be taught.

- Oscar Wilde

*

The great universal family of men is a utopia worthy of the most mediocre logic.

— Comte de Lautreamont

*

It is like information theory; it is noise posing as signal, so you do not even recognize it as noise. The intelligence agencies call it disinformation. If you can float enough disinformation into circulation, you will totally abolish everyone's contact with reality, probably your own included.

— Philip K. Dick

*

Conservative is not clinging on to yesterday, conservative is living by the principles that have always been valid.

— Antoine de Rivarol

*

Tradition is not something constant but the product of a process of selection guided not by reason but by success.

— Friedrich Hayek

*

Liberals claim to want to give a hearing to other views, but then are shocked and offended to discover that there are other views.

— William F. Buckley, Jr.

*

The further fascism recedes into history and the fewer visible fascists there are on display, the more self-proclaimed anti-fascists need fascism to retain any semblance of political virtue or purpose.

— Douglas Murray

*

Why has government been instituted at all? Because the passions of man will not conform to the dictates of reason and justice without constraint.

— Alexander Hamilton

*

Intellectuals, in the words of the writer Eric Hoffer, "cannot operate at room temperature." They are excited by daring opinions, clever theories, sweeping ideologies, and utopian visions of the kind that caused so much trouble during the 20th century. The kind of reason that expands moral sensibilities comes not from grand intellectual "systems" but from the exercise of logic, clarity, objectivity, and proportionality.

— Steven Pinker

*

A doctrine must not be understood, but has rather to be believed in. We can be absolutely certain only about things we do not understand. A doctrine that is understood is shorn of its strength. Once we understand a thing, it is as if it had originated in us. And, clearly, those who are asked to renounce the self and sacrifice it cannot see eternal certitude in anything which originates in that self.

— Eric Hoffer

*

The difference between Greek pessimism and the oriental and modern variety is that the Greeks had not made the discovery that the pathetic mood may be idealized, and figure as a higher form of sensibility. Their spirit was still too essentially masculine for pessimism to be elaborated or lengthily dwelt on in their classic literature... The discovery that the enduring emphasis, so far as this world goes, may be laid on its pain and failure, was reserved for races more complex, and (so to speak) more feminine than the Hellenes had attained to being in the classic period.

— William James

*

Today's parents dwell uncomfortably and self-consciously in the all-too-powerful shadow of the adolescent ethos of the 1960s, a decade whose excesses led to a general denigration of adulthood, an unthinking disbelief in the existence of competent power, and the inability to distinguish between the chaos of immaturity and responsible freedom.

— Jordan B. Peterson

*

Results matter - they are the ultimate justification of processes - but it is only the general effectiveness of particular processes (competitive markets, constitutional government) that can be gauged by man, not each individual result in isolation.

— Thomas Sowell

Either you are a feminist, or you are a sexist/misogynist. There is no box marked 'other.'

— Ani DiFranco

*

Feminists often pretend to be angry and offended in order to win debates or, I should say, prevent debates from ever happening. If you can act angry and offended, especially on a college campus, you can shut down the other side using a speech code.

— Mike Adams

*

Personally, I'm not a feminist, as I can't stand puritans.

— Vivienne Westwood

*

Social justice is the atrocious principle that implies all rewards should be determined by political power.

— Friedrich Hayek

*

The government cannot love you, and any politics that works on a different assumption is destined for no good.

— Jonah Goldberg

*

Only the individual thinks. Only the individual reasons. Only the Individual Acts.

— Ludwig von Mises

*

I don't want to run your life. I don't know how to run your life. I don't have the authority to run your life. And the Constitution doesn't permit me to run your life.

— Ron Paul

*

Horror and terror lurk behind the walls provided so wisely by our ancestors. We tear them down at our own peril.

— Jordan B. Peterson

*

Every reform movement has a lunatic fringe.

— Theodore Roosevelt

*

A plain husband-man is more Prudent in the affairs of his own house, than a Privy Counselor in the affairs of other men.

— Thomas Hobbes

*

I mean, I've always been a libertarian. Leave everybody alone. Let everybody else do what they want. Just stay out of everybody else's hair.

— Clint Eastwood

*

Liberals have invented whole college majors - psychology, sociology and women's studies - to prove that nothing is anybody's fault.

— P. J. O'Rourke

*

A government big enough to give you everything you want is a government big enough to take from you everything you have.

— Gerald R. Ford

*

Compared with the totality of knowledge continually utilized in the evolution of a dynamic civilization, the difference between the knowledge that the wisest and that which the most ignorant individual can deliberately employ is comparatively insignificant.

— Friedrich Hayek

*

Communism doesn't work because people like to own stuff.

— Frank Zappa

*

I don't trust liberals, I trust conservatives.

— Lucius Annaeus Seneca

*

The most terrifying words in the English language are I'm from the government and I'm here to help.

— Ronald Reagan

About the Author

Dazed and confused about Germany in general and Berlin in particular, Hermann Observer (aka Clarsonimus Maximus) is a mean, cynical and nasty old expatriate American who observes the world around him in quiet desperation.

You can visit me at Observing Hermann.

You can contact me at clarsonimus@aol.com.

I tweet my Twitter tweet stuff at @clarsonimus.

"To read too many books is harmful." But try one of these anyway.

Brain Quest
Dumb Deutsch
The Little Red Book
501 German Oddities
The Sayings of Confusius
The Media Mind Manipulation Manual

You can visit him at Observing Hermann.
You can contact him at clarsonimus@aol.com.
He tweets his Twitter tweet stuff at @clarsonimus.

Brain Quest - A Fantastic Voyage through the Progressive Mind:

Mission Nemo simply must succeed. If the crew of the Super Small Miniaturized Nano-like Operations Wessel S. S. Minnow fails to destroy the inoperable anti-capitalist coagulum lodged in Maurice Moore's progressive brain, how will General De Klein's Federal Department of Antidotes operatives at SUCFACE Mission Control find out if Leftylometazoline (aka LeftX) really works? Would this usher in the final stage of the liberal clerisy's clandestine collectivist conspiracy to abolish our few remaining individual freedoms forever? That would not please President Thump one microscopic little bit.

Join Major Miles Stone and his disturbingly alluring crew on their miniaturized mission through the left and lefter hemispheres of the progressive brain. Their fantastic voyage is a race against time that takes them through such redoubtable regions as the Clinton Vortex, the Che Guevara Gray Area and the Obama Trauma Center itself. Here they bravely confront such anatomical monstrosities as the fantasist frontalis, the hyperbolthalamus and the dreaded pious aspiration node. Their progressive brain journey only gets progressively worse as they are repeatedly attacked by repulsive swarms of nanny neurons, doomsday dendrons, robin hoodlums and the formidable radical egalitarian bacterium. If not for the courage of the fearless crew, and their deadly arsenal of passing phasers, millennial mindset missiles, moral busybody antibodies and Condescendium®, the Minnow would be lost. The Minnow would be lost.

The tension never stops building during this thrilling tale of adventure, danger, suspense and romance. And lust. Will Captain Hanna Grenada's irresistible animal magnetism finally seduce the Major into experiencing something vaguely resembling basic human emotion? Can the all too communicative HAL 9999 super computer and his annoying eye drones really be trusted to operate the ship? And will the Minnow's political corrector deflectors and smug shields hold, allowing Stone and his crew to reach their target and ignite the liberal bombast bomb in time? I could tell you but that would ruin the suspense.

Not your everyday dystopian science-fiction erotic horror political thriller, this bombastic bombshell of a book knows no shame when it comes to overwhelming you with its serious silliness, wanton wackiness and forthright, flat-out farce. Purchase it now before it is too late or something. Soon to be made into a major motion picture. Or maybe it has been already. There is also time travel involved here, after all.

*

501 German Oddities - Observations from an Innocent Abroad:

Sure you may have thought that you already knew everything there was to know about Germany and the Germans. Every school child knows that Germany is the land of circulatory disorders, Döner Kebab, naked sledding competitions and David Hasselhoff. But Germany is more than that. Much more. Did you know, for instance, that Germans invented the *"Volkswagen,"* brew over 5000 types of a popular drink called "*Bier*" and were actively involved in World War II? I didn't think so. That is why I have gone to the great trouble of putting an enormous amount of my precious time and effort into compiling a work of literary and socio-historical "*Kunst*" that will now fill in some of those appalling gaps of knowledge you have.

This stupendously superficial and yet "*Supergeil*" seminal study will thrill you with its humorous ranting, incisive raving and profound collection of unpremeditated observations, crude commentary and unsolicited opinion, all presented to you by an accomplished "*Deutschland*" expert with over 30 years of active experience in "*das Feld*," most of which having taken place in the baffling and bewildering city of "*Berlin*" itself (I was actually referring to me when citing that expert guy there).

This is "*ein gutes Buch*" and I can only hope that you will enjoy reading it half as much as I have enjoyed getting read of it (that was a pun), as in finally getting all of this pent-up aggression and frustration off my chest, I mean. The names have been changed to protect the innocent. What you see is what you get. It takes two to tango. You can lead a horse to water but you can't make him drink. You can't judge a book by its cover. Well, in this case maybe you can. But have a good laugh and *"Viel Spaß dabei"* anyway.

*

Dumb Deutsch - Absurd German Language Errors (auch für deutsche Leser geeignet):

Have you ever ordered leather cheese? Have you ever told your cab driver that your hotel is located on One-Way Street? I doubt it. But English speakers trying to speak German say bizarre things like this all the time and I, for one, feel their pain. Acutely, even. They are speaking Dumb Deutsch. And they have no one else to blame but themselves.

It is not that those of us who speak Dumb Deutsch actually intend to say the embarrassing and dumbfounding things we do. It doesn't matter what we intend to do. It is inevitable. And it became inevitable the moment we decided to start speaking "that awful German language" in the first place. And please note the fine distinction here: Although very closely related, German and Dumb Deutsch are two entirely different languages.

The German language is complex, treacherous and terribly difficult to learn. It has three sexes, for crying out loud. It has four or five or maybe even six cases (I forget). It is full of pitfalls, perils, strange idioms and ludicrous aphorisms. There are always one or two super-important exceptions for every iron-clad grammatical rule given. There are insanely long words and even longer sentences, compound words that get chopped up and tossed around indiscriminately and unimaginable word combinations that native German speakers seemingly construct and then discard again at will. Then you have those tricky nuances and complex distinctions, the false friends, the twisted

Anglicisms, the weird breathing noises and all of those quaint expressions alluding to pigs and shit.

Dumb Deutsch, on the other hand, is relatively straightforward and can be learned in about fifteen minutes. This is because Dumb Deutsch speakers are completely unaware of all of those pesky German language complexities just listed above. And this is of course also why when it is spoken correctly, as in incorrectly, Dumb Deutsch is a never-ending source of confusion, mirth, shame, shock and horror for the German captive audience being forced to listen to it.

So please sit back and enjoy this short collection of bloodcurdling blunders, frightful faux pas and grisly gaffes, all in the Dumb Deutsch original. Many of these were mistakes I made all on my own. Many more have been contributed by friends and acquaintances. Numerous others were found surfing the Internet and reading about them elsewhere.

For the sake of fairness, a number of ridiculous errors Germans make when trying to speak English have also been included.

Bitte beachten: Diese Sammlung von peinlichen Ausrutschern und haarsträubenden Fehltritten ist selbstverständlich auch für deutsche Leser geeignet.

*

The Sayings of Confusius - Confusionism for Beginners:

Confusius is confused. He is confused about cultural appropriation, for instance. He is also confused about gender fluidity, identity politics, Cancel Culture and the Diversity Cult. Left-wing bullies, Marxist intellectuals, Antifa, Extinction Rebellion and Greta Thunberg confuse him. Postmodern academics and their social constructionism and deconstructionism confuse him. He is confused about Social Justice warriors and kindred progressive activists. "Woke" people who are clearly sound asleep confuse him. All the systemic problems in American society that aren't systemic confuse him. Radical feminism, intersectionality, essentialism and otherness confuse him. Microaggression and safe spaces confuse him. Unsolicited Hollywood celebrity opinions confuse him, just like phony oppression and victimhood. Uncontrolled immigration confuses him. BLM, ANTIFA, DNC, AOC, LGBTQ, WMCMH, NGO, UN, EU, FBI, D.C. and many others confuse him. Progressive platitudes confuse him. Vindictiveness in general and political correctness in particular confuses him. Internationalism, left-wing overreach, liberal domination in education, academia and our extraordinarily biased mainstream media confuse him. Particularly confusing is watching how his fellow citizens, many of them confused just like him, let themselves be patronized, harassed and silenced by all of the above. Most confusing of all, however, is that The Great Presidential Election Fraud of 2020 could have taken place in the United States of America. Confusius feels as if the world has just been pulled out from beneath his feet and is genuinely astonished at the next level of confusion we are all currently witnessing in the White House.

Confusionism is an expression of this confusion and the assorted observations which make up this little book are an attempt to come to grips with the demoralization we are now observing all around us. It is a spontaneous reaction to the turmoil that permeates what remains of the civil society we once lived in. Like the conservatism it stems from, confusionism is not a philosophy per se but a response to the excesses of left-wing lunacy. It is an attempt to illustrate the senselessness of liberal "anything goes" culture now masquerading as the norm in American society. It is a quiet rebellion against the status quo of leftist ideological politics and the bludgeon of moral condescension progressives use against anyone of us who refuses to be indoctrinated. Like a cry for help in the wilderness that may never be heard, confusionism is nevertheless a cry of hope. A rather confused cry of hope, granted, but a cry of hope all the same. The hope is that the disregard for fairness, justice, honesty and objectivity we are now witnessing first-hand can somehow be checked and eventually undone.

And just who is Confusius? I am not at liberty to tell you. He insists that his identity be kept a secret. All I can say for sure is that he is even more emotionally unstable than before the election took place and has become obsessed with subjecting complete strangers like yourself to his boorish confusionist views, "jokes" and unsolicited advice. I can also tell you that he is not Chinese, even though he insists on expressing himself with an amateurish, hokey faux-Chinese accent and a ridiculous grammatical style he probably assumes to be Chinese as well. He specifically asked me to pass on to you his heartfelt wish that you enjoy this collection of confusionist erudition. He also asks that you never forget, should you share his confusion, that hope is being able to see that there is light despite all of the darkness.

*

The Media Mind Manipulation Manual - What Journalists Must Know to Keep Their Sheeple under Control:

There's a lot to be said about the world's second oldest profession. Unfortunately, not much of it is very good. Let's face it, journalism leaves a bad taste in your mouth. And The Media Mind Manipulation Manual (MMMM) will help you understand why that is. It's the ultimate guide for journalism as it was never meant to be - the fraudulent and corrupt journalism that journalism has become today.

There is a lot to be said about the world's second oldest profession. Unfortunately, not much of it is very good. Let's face it, journalism leaves a bad taste in your mouth. Watch five minutes of mainstream media if you don't believe me (and keep your toothbrush handy). It's not just that journalists are amoral opportunists who refuse to respect even the most basic ethical norms. They're also cynical swindlers and deceitful hypocrites incapable of moral judgement. Many, of course, are also conniving, money-grubbing hacks who lack even an ounce of integrity. But having said that, I'm sure many of you are nevertheless asking yourselves how you too could become successful media hacks. After all, having a guaranteed customer base and income, unlimited social prestige and power and no ethical considerations to speak of, who could ask for more? Well, you've come to the right place. After many years of comprehensive research, I offer you now the Media Mind Manipulation Manual, or MMMM for short. It's a unique collection of valuable tips, tricks, tactics and techniques that will help you streamline your shameless spin and heighten your hysterical hype. Seasoned journalists will also benefit from this invaluable guide, taking advantage of the many cutting-edge deceptive journalistic methods and practices now out on the street. There's something for everyone here. The Media Mind Manipulation Manual is the ultimate guide for journalism as it was never meant to be - the fraudulent and corrupt journalism that journalism has become today. May this manual serve you well.

www.ingramcontent.com/pod-product-compliance
Lightning Source LLC
Chambersburg PA
CBHW051357280526
45784CB00007B/2999